BEGINNING MOZART FOR PIANO

Boston Music Company

Published by
Boston Music Company

Exclusive Distributors:
Hal Leonard
7777 West Bluemound Road, Milwaukee, WI 53213
Email: info@halleonard.com

Hal Leonard Europe Limited
42 Wigmore Street Maryleborne, London, WIU 2 RY
Email: info@halleonardeurope.com

Hal Leonard Australia Pty. Ltd.
4 Lentara Court Cheltenham, Victoria, 9132 Australia
Email: info@halleonard.com.au

Order No. BM12298
ISBN 1-84609-744-4

This book © Copyright 2006 & 2007
Boston Music Company

Series Editor David Harrison.
Music edited by Rachel Payne & Sam Harrop.
Cover designed by Michael Bell Design.

For all works contained herein:
Unauthorized copying, arranging, adapting, recording, Internet posting,
public performance, or other distribution of the music in this publication is an infringement of copyright.
Infringers are liable under the law.

Printed in EU.

www.halleonard.com

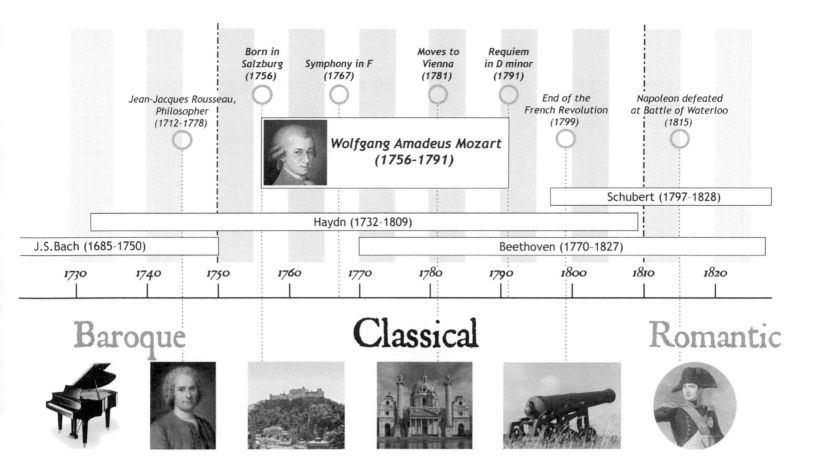

Baroque   Classical   Romantic

Wolfgang Amadeus Mozart was born in Salzburg, Austria, on 27 January 1756 and, though he lived a short life, was to become one of the most influential composers of all time.

Mozart's musicianship began at a staggeringly young age; he was picking out tunes by ear as a toddler and had begun writing pieces by the age of five. His teacher was his father Leopold – a composer, violinist and theorist who recognised his son's gifts and took both him and his similarly gifted daughter, Maria Anna, on grand tours throughout Europe to display their prodigious talents.

After these tours Mozart returned to Salzburg in 1766. Mozart's output greatly increased from this point, despite having already written many compositions. In 1773, at the age of just seventeen, Mozart was formally employed as Konzertmeister at the Salzburg court. Here he was to be given the opportunity to compose in many styles, including symphonies, sonatas, string quartets and operas. By 1777 Mozart had composed nearly 300 works including over 20 symphonies.

Mozart grew more and more discontented with the lack of opportunities to further his musical career in Salzburg and in late 1777 set off on travels with his mother, who died during their time in Paris. Although this death terribly affected Mozart, over the subsequent months he continued his European travels in search of work. He was unsuccessful in this regard and, in 1779, his father ordered his return to Salzburg where he had arranged a superior post at the court.

In 1781 Mozart was summoned to Vienna by his employer, Prince-Archbishop Colloredo of Salzburg. Mozart quickly became unhappy with his treatment by Colloredo and resigned to become a freelance musician. Mozart's output consequently increased and he wrote some of his greatest piano concertos, symphonies and operas. Whilst in Vienna Mozart also became good friends with Haydn, who made no secret of his admiration for Mozart. He famously declared to Leopold Mozart, 'Before God and as an honest man, your son is the greatest composer known to me'.

Between 1782 and 1785, Mozart had focused much of his attention on piano compositions, but in 1786 more operas emerged and *The Marriage of Figaro* was composed and premiered. *Don Giovanni* soon followed to great acclaim.

Mozart's financial situation steadily declined towards the end of the 1780s as he appeared less frequently in public concerts – he and his family moved from central Vienna to the suburbs and he began to borrow money to travel to Germany in an effort to improve his fortunes.

He died in 1791, probably from rheumatic fever, but his output did not slow in his last year. *The Magic Flute*, *Clarinet Concerto in A*, and his *Requiem* (which remained unfinished at his death) were all written in his last year. By this point Mozart had shown his compositional mastery and had written the greatest operas of his age. His influence stretched far and wide within his own lifetime and also well into the centuries that followed his death. His iconic status remains today.

Adagio

Slow Movement from Clarinet Concerto, K622

© Copyright 2006, by the Boston Music Co.
All Rights Reserved. International Copyright Secured.

Minuet in C Major

Andante grazioso

© Copyright 2006, by the Boston Music Co.
All Rights Reserved. International Copyright Secured.

Contredanse in G Major

With movement

© Copyright 2006, by the Boston Music Co.
All Rights Reserved. International Copyright Secured.

Eine Kleine Nachtmusik, K525

Ist Movement: Allegro

Allegro

© Copyright 2006, by the Boston Music Co.
All Rights Reserved. International Copyright Secured.

Ave Verum Corpus, K618

Not too slow

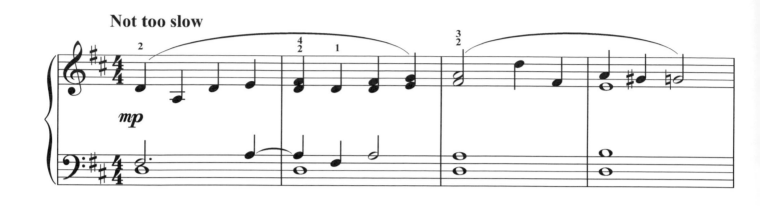

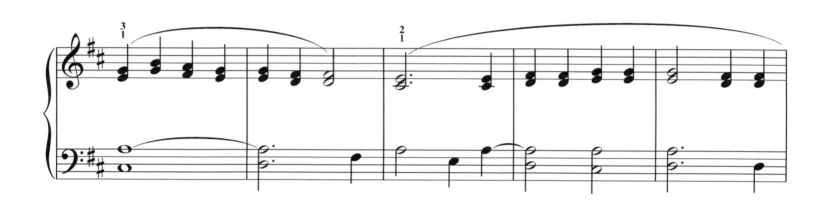

© Copyright 2006, by the Boston Music Co.
All Rights Reserved. International Copyright Secured.

Minuet in F Major

© Copyright 2006, by the Boston Music Co.
All Rights Reserved. International Copyright Secured.

German Dance

'The Sleigh Ride'

© Copyright 2006, by the Boston Music Co.
All Rights Reserved. International Copyright Secured.

Allegro in B♭ Major

Allegro giocoso

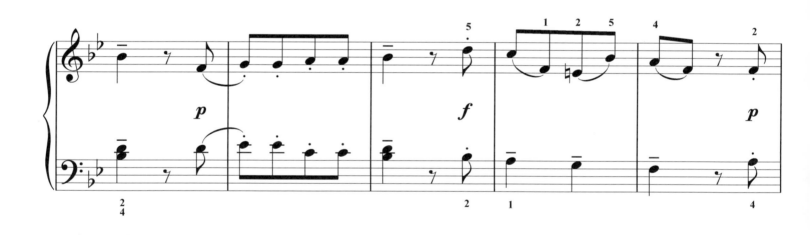

© Copyright 2006, by the Boston Music Co.
All Rights Reserved. International Copyright Secured.

Symphony No. 40 (Theme)

Molto Allegro

© Copyright 2006, by the Boston Music Co.
All Rights Reserved. International Copyright Secured.

Contredanse in A Major

© Copyright 2006, by the Boston Music Co.
All Rights Reserved. International Copyright Secured.

Air in E♭ Major

Andantino

© Copyright 2006, by the Boston Music Co.
All Rights Reserved. International Copyright Secured.

Minuet and Trio

from Symphony in F, K43

Moderately

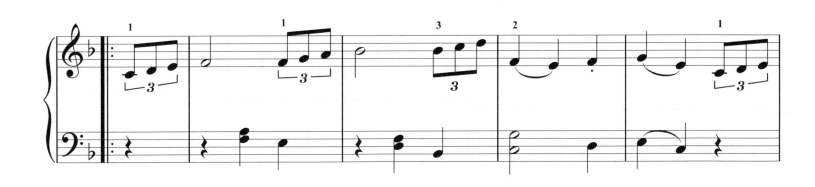

Fine

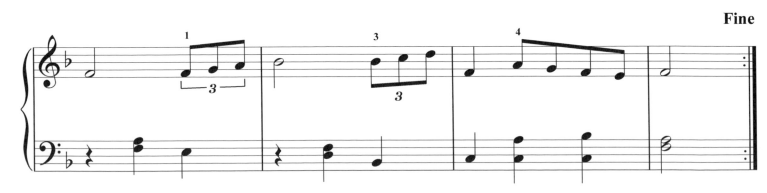

© Copyright 2006, by the Boston Music Co.
All Rights Reserved. International Copyright Secured.

Trio

D.C. Minuet

19

Romance

from Eine Kleine Nachtmusik, K525

Slowly

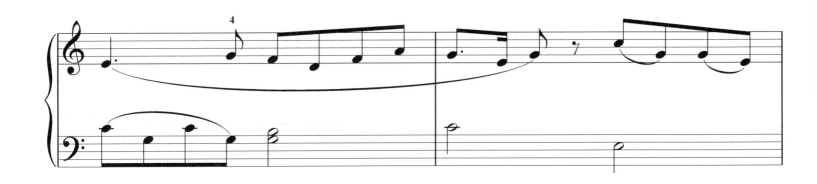

© Copyright 2006, by the Boston Music Co.
All Rights Reserved. International Copyright Secured.

Minuet

from Don Giovanni

Tempo di minuetto

© Copyright 2006, by the Boston Music Co.
All Rights Reserved. International Copyright Secured.

Là ci darem la mano

from Don Giovanni

Andante

© Copyright 2006, by the Boston Music Co.
All Rights Reserved. International Copyright Secured.

Andante in E♭ Major

© Copyright 2006, by the Boston Music Co.
All Rights Reserved. International Copyright Secured.

Duettino in A♭ Major

© Copyright 2006, by the Boston Music Co.
All Rights Reserved. International Copyright Secured.

Andantino in E♭ Major, K236

© Copyright 2006, by the Boston Music Co.
All Rights Reserved. International Copyright Secured.

Theme and Three Variations, K265

'Ah! Vous dirai-je, Maman'

Theme

© Copyright 2006, by the Boston Music Co.
All Rights Reserved. International Copyright Secured.

Var. 3

'Sonata Facile' in C Major (Theme)

Allegro

© Copyright 2006, by the Boston Music Co.
All Rights Reserved. International Copyright Secured.

Andante Grazioso (Theme)

from Piano Sonata in A, K331

Andante grazioso

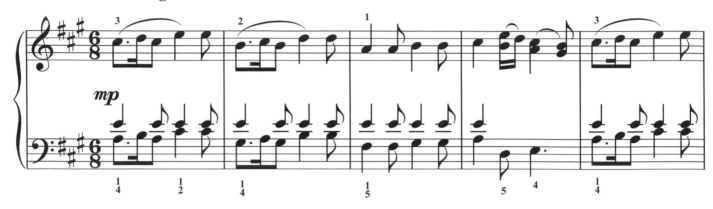

© Copyright 2006, by the Boston Music Co.
All Rights Reserved. International Copyright Secured.